This step by step book
belong to

To

_____

_____

Copyright © 2020 by Happy Turtle Press

All rights reserved.

No part of this book may be reproduced in any form or by any electronic or mechanical means, including information storage and retrieval systems, without written permission from the author, except for the use of brief quotations in a book review.

About Us

Happy Turtle Press is a family-owned publishing press by Alex and Jessica based in Seattle, WA.

The origin of "HTP" came when Alex was just 12 years old…

It was a cold December day when Alex had his first anxiety attack in the 6th grade.

The teachers didn't know what happened, and he was rushed to the emergency room out of panic.

"Everything will be okay", the doctor said, "but he will need to get on anxiety medicine".

"Anxiety medicine? He's 12", Alex's mom said.

Reluctantly, Alex was put on anxiety medicine. And after months of being on it, it didn't work.

Alex was losing his focus, his attention span, and was still stressed out.

It wasn't until Alex's mother bought him multiple coloring and activity books did things change.

With a daily practice of using coloring and activity books, within weeks, Alex began to remain calm, and increase his focus like never before.

Alex soon went off the medication (within doctor's approval), and things got better.

That year, Alex became one of the highest-grade earners, and even spoke as "mini valedictorian" during the promotion ceremony.

Alex thanks coloring and activity books for his success in life.

He and his wife now are on a journey to create coloring books that will impact the lives of young children like his 12-year-old self.

Each book is put through an intensive review system where at least 50 real parents test and review the activity book. After that, revisions are made and sent out to a new set of testers for final approval. Finally, the book is ready for you and your family.

Each masterpiece is a gift from our family to yours.

We hope you love your new book as much as we do!

How To Draw Stag Deer

1

2

3

4

5

How To Draw Turkey

1.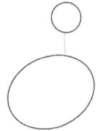
2.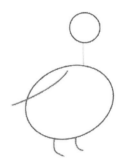
3.
4.
5.

HOW TO DRAW PRAIRIE RATTLESNAKE

HOW TO DRAW RED FOX

HOW TO DRAW GRAY SQUIRREL

1
2
3
4
5

How To Draw Forest elephant

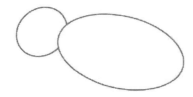

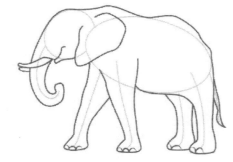

HOW TO DRAW BIGHORN SHEEP

How To Draw Bobcat

1

2
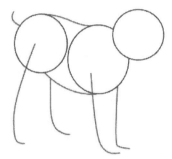

3
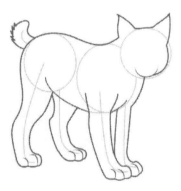

4

5

HOW TO DRAW CUTTHROAT TROUT

1
2
3
4
5

How To Draw Bison

1)
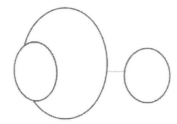

2)
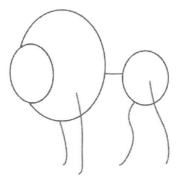

3)
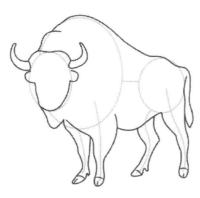

4)

5)

HOW TO DRAW BARN OWL

1
2
3
4
5

How To Draw Bald eagle

1
2
3
4
5

How To Draw Mute swan

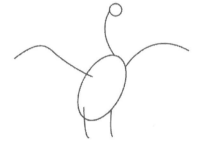

How To Draw Beaver

1
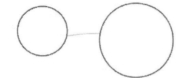

2

3

4

5

How To Draw Mountain lion

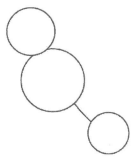

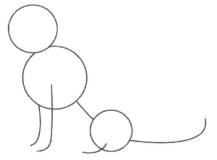

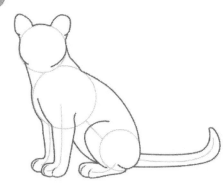

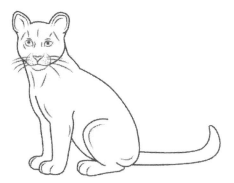

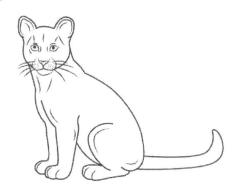

How To Draw Orangutan

1།

2།

3།

4།

5།

HOW TO DRAW GRIZZLY BEAR

1.

2.

3.

4.

5.

How To Draw Stag Deer

1

2

3

4

5

How To Draw Coyote

1.

2.

3.
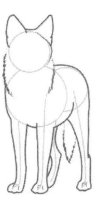

4.

5.

HOW TO DRAW GREY WOLF

How To Draw Rocky mountain

HOW TO DRAW MOOSE

1

2
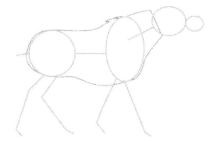

3
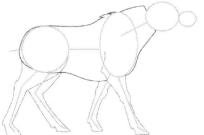

4
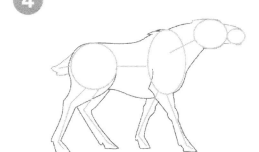

5

HOW TO DRAW RACCOON

HOW TO DRAW CUTTHROAT TROUT

1

2
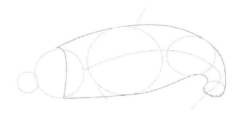

3
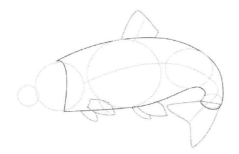

4
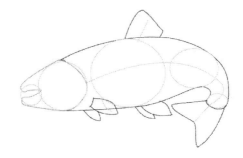

5
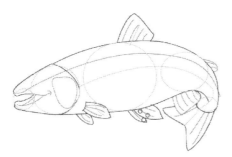

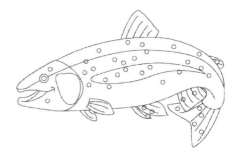

HOW TO DRAW FAWN

HOW TO DRAW CHIPMUNK

1.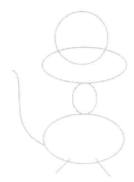
2.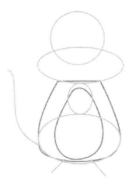
3.
4.
5.

HOW TO DRAW HEDGEHOG

Made in the USA
Coppell, TX
07 June 2020